HOW FO' SURF

WIT' PALAKA JOE

AN' NO TEEZ DA SPELLING!

by Patrick Ching and Jeff Pagay
Introduction by Rell Sunn

ALOHA, I'm Rell Sunn.

Surfing is the most wonderful sport in the world; any surfer will tell you that . . . but it isn't easy to learn. I have a good friend who is an expert mountain climber, fly-fisherman, and all-around outdoor sportsman; he's also been a hardcore surfer for forty years. Recently he told me that of all the sports in the world, surfing was by far the most difficult to learn.

Like Palaka Joe says in this book, the best thing about surfing is, "only get one rule . . . **NO MO' RULES!**" But there **are** rules in surfing: they're just unwritten rules. Surfing has an incredibly rich culture and heritage, and a complicated system of etiquette. Surf lore has mostly been passed on verbally from one generation to the next, by talkin' story or plunking on the 'ukulele. That's why this book is so delightful; its hapa-pidgin and humor is straight off the beach, but the information is 'solid' and fun for even the most 'read-aphobic' surfer.

I love books and reading; when I couldn't afford to travel I would pick up a book about Africa or Australia and try to imagine what it would be like to be there with a surfboard someday. If you can't get there, if your hair is dry and your surfboard dusty, then read the book.

'Kay-den!

Rell

FOR FREE SURF FLICK: FLICK PAGE CORNERS FROM BACK TO FRONT!

HOWZIT!!?

I'M PALAKA JOE.

Y'KNOW, THERE'S NOTHIN' LIKE DA FEELIN' OF BEING CARRIED ACROSS THE OCEAN'S SUR- FACE BY A WAVE. FEW THINGS CAN BRING YOU MORE EXCITEMENT, TRANQUILITY, AND GRAT- IFICATION THAN SURFING.

HAVING GROWN UP IN THE HAWAIIAN SURF, I'VE ACQUIRED THE ATTITUDE AND SKILLS WHICH ENABLE ME TO TEACH THE ART OF SURFING TO EVEN THE MOST HOPELESS LŌLŌS.

I'LL TRY TO SPEAK GOOD ENGLISH, BUT IF I GET CARRIED AWAY, TRY TO UNDERSTAND, I BEEN TALKING LIKE DIS MA' WHOLE LIFE. THERE'S A GLOSSARY IN BACK IF YOU' REALLY CLUELESS.

YOU KNOW, WITH ALL SURFING HAS TO OFFER, DA TING I LIKE MOST ABOUT IT IS

... ONLY GET ONE RULE ...

SO YOU WANNA LEARN HOW FO' SURF?

WELL, BEFORE WE PADDLE OUT IN THOSE TWENTY FOOTERS, LET'S BACK UP A BIT AND LEARN SOMETHING ABOUT WHAT WE'RE GETTING INTO . . .

THE HAWAIIAN WORD FOR SURF IS **NALU.** BOARD SURFING, OR **HE'E NALU,** WAS PIONEERED IN HAWAI'I HUNDREDS OF YEARS AGO. IT WAS THE FAVORITE SPORT OF MANY HAWAIIAN CHIEFS INCLUDING KAMEHAMEHA THE GREAT. SINCE THEN SURFING HAS BECOME POPULAR WORLDWIDE BUT HAS RETAINED THE REPUTATION AS "THE SPORT OF KINGS." INDEED, GLIDING EFFORTLESSLY ALONG THE FACE OF A WAVE CAN MAKE ANYONE FEEL LIKE ROYALTY!

PAPA HE'E NALU IS THE HAWAIIAN NAME FOR SURFBOARD. IN ANCIENT TIMES THE BOARDS WERE MADE FROM VARIOUS WOODS INCLUDING **'ULU** (BREADFRUIT), **KOA** (ACACIA), AND THE MOST PRIZED **WILIWILI** (HAWAIIAN CORAL TREE). SOME OF THOSE BOARDS MEASURED NEARLY TWENTY FEET LONG AND WEIGHED ALMOST 200 POUNDS!

THE GREAT WATERMAN, DUKE KAHANAMOKU, MADE LEGENDARY RIDES USING A STREAMLINED VERSION OF THE ANCIENT BOARDS. THESE BOARDS WERE USUALLY SHAPED OF HOLLOWED OUT RED-WOOD AND WEIGHED ABOUT 50 POUNDS.

THE DAWN OF MODERN SURFING BEGAN IN THE 1940'S WITH THE INTRODUCTION OF BALSA AND FIBERGLASS BOARDS FIT-TED WITH A FIN OR "SKEG." THESE WERE FOLLOWED IN THE LATE 1950'S BY FOAM AND FIBERGLASS BOARDS WHICH ARE THE STANDARD TODAY. THESE NEW BOARDS ENABLE RIDERS TO MANEUVER THROUGH WAVES LIKE NEVER BEFORE.

THE BEST PART IS THESE BOARDS WEIGH LESS THAN A NĀNĀKULI ROOF-RAT!

SINGLE-FIN TWIN-FIN TRY-FIN "TRUSTA"

RECENT DECADES HAVE WITNESSED DRASTIC CHANGES IN SURFBOARD DESIGN. VARIATIONS IN SHAPES, ALONG WITH FIN SIZE AND NUMBER OF FINS, HAVE REVOLUTIONIZED THE SURFING INDUSTRY.

BY RIDING VARIOUS KINDS OF BOARDS YOU WILL DISCOVER WHAT SHAPES AND SIZES WORK BEST FOR YOU. WHO KNOWS, MAYBE SOMEDAY YOU'LL BE SHAPING YOUR **OWN** CUSTOM BOARDS.

PARTS OF A SURFBOARD

NOSE

RAIL
(ROLLED EDGE)

STRINGER
(WOODEN STRIP
WITHIN FOAM)

ROCKER
(UPWARD CURVE
OF NOSE)

DECK
(TOP SURFACE)

BOTTOM

CHANNELS
(DESIGN OPTION)

STINGER
(POPULAR IN 70'S)

FIN
OR
SKEG

TAIL

WING

NOSE AND TAIL SHAPES

NEEDLE-NOSE

ROUND-NOSE

PIN-TAIL

SWALLOW-TAIL

SQUASH-TAIL

SURF GEAR

BOARD RACKS — MAY BE BUILT, BOUGHT OR BORROWED.
HINT: DON'T FORGET TO STRAP THEM ON.

CAR — ANY MAKE, MODEL OR CONDITION WILL DO. DOORS AND ROOF OPTIONAL.

JUGS OF WATER — FOR DRINKING, WASHING STUFF OFF, OR REFILLING RADIATORS.

WAX — THIS HELPS YOU TO STICK TO YOUR SURFBOARD. RUB IT ON YOUR BOARD — NOT YOUR BODY.

GLASSES — *ANY KINE AWRIGHT. WHATEVER MAKES YOU LOOK COOL.*

SURFBOARD — *ESSENTIAL EQUIPMENT FOR BOARD SURFING.*

LEASH, CORD — *KEEPS BOARD FROM GETTING SWEPT IN AFTER A WIPEOUT. ALSO HELPS TO LOCATE MISSING SURFERS.*

SHORTS — *STYLES COME AND GO. **WARNING:** GET THE KIND THAT STAY ON.*

SLIPPA'S — *IN HAOLE: THONGS, SHOES, FLIP FLOPS, SLAPS. WHATEVA', PUT 'EM ON YO' FEET.
IT IS CUSTOMARY TO REMOVE SLIPPA'S BEFORE ENTERING OCEAN.

MUTT — *SOMETHING TO PROTECT YOUR GEAR, ATTRACT BABES, AND EAT LEFTOVERS.*

ANATOMY

RIGHTS

MOST WAVES ARE GENERATED BY STORMS OUT AT SEA. THE WAVES TRAVEL ACROSS THE OCEAN IN GROUPS OR **"SETS."** AS THE SETS OF WAVES REACH SHALLOW WATER THEY PITCH OUT OR **"BREAK."**

JUST BEFORE A WAVE BREAKS IT IS AT ITS HIGHTEST POINT OR **"PEAK."** DA **"LIP"** IS THE EDGE OF THE WAVE THAT IS IN THE PROCESS OF THROWING OVER. DA **"PIT"** IS WHERE THE LIP IS LANDING. IT IS THE MOST DANGEROUS PART OF THE WAVE. AS IT THROWS OVER, THE WAVE MAY FORM A **"TUBE."**

THE **"WHITEWASH"** IS ANY PART OF THE WAVE THAT HAS ALREADY BROKEN. THE **"SHOULDER"** IS LOCATED AT THE END OF THE WAVE THAT HAS NOT BROKEN. IN SOME LOCATIONS A **"BOWL"** IS FORMED BETWEEN THE TUBE AND THE SHOULDER OF A WAVE. A GOOD EXAMPLE OF THIS IS THE FAMOUS "ALA MOANA BOWL."

THE SPEED AND DIRECTION OF THE WIND WILL DETERMINE THE *"CONDITIONS"* IN WHICH A WAVE BREAKS. LIGHT *"OFFSHORE WINDS"* PRODUCE A *"GLASSY"* SURFACE AND FORM NICE HOLLOW TUBES. STRONG *"ONSHORE WINDS"* WILL CREATE *"CHOPPY"* CONDITIONS TURNING THE WAVES TO *"MUSH."*

THE DIRECTION OF A WAVE IS DETERMINED BY WHICH WAY IT BREAKS AS YOU FACE TOWARD SHORE. IF YOU'RE LOOKING AT THE WAVES *FROM* SHORE, JUS' REMEMBER THAT *LEFTS IS RIGHT* AND *RIGHTS IS LEFT.*

IN HAWAI'I, WAVES ARE OFTEN REFERRED TO AS *"BREAKS." "FIRST BREAKS"* ARE THE FARTHEST OUT WHILE *SECOND, THIRD* OR *"INSIDE BREAKS"* ARE CLOSER TO SHORE.

WHEN A WAVE BREAKS, ITS FRONT OR *"FACE"* MAY BE TWICE AS TALL AS ITS *"BACK."* HERE IN HAWAI'I, WE JUDGE THE SIZE OF A WAVE BY THE HEIGHT OF ITS BACK. SO A THREE FOOT WAVE MAY HAVE A FACE MEASURING SIX FEET HIGH.

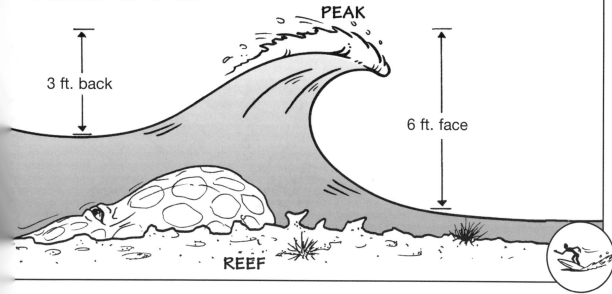

ARE YOU READY FOR YOUR FIRST LESSON IN SURFING?

EH LŌLŌ, MAKE SURE YOU CAN SWIM FIRST AH!

FIRST TIME SURFERS ARE OFTEN SURPRISED AT HOW HARD IT IS JUST TO SIT ON A SURFBOARD. (SHORTER BOARDS ARE ESPECIALLY SQUIRMY.) AT FIRST, JUST TRY TO FIND YOUR SPOT IN THE SITTING POSITION. AFTER A WHILE YOU'LL FEEL MORE COMFORTABLE AS YOUR BODY BEGINS TO DISCOVER THE MOST IMPORTANT THING ABOUT SURFING . . . **BALANCE.**

MANY WOULD BE SURFERS NEVER GET PAST THE LEARNING STAGE BECAUSE OF THE EMBARRASSMENT. PUT IT ASIDE! REMEMBER, EVERYBODY WHO SURFS WAS A BEGINNER AT ONE TIME.

THEN THERE'S THE PAIN. EVEN AN OLYMPIC ATHLETE WILL FEEL HIS MUSCLES TIGHTEN AND BURN IF HE ISN'T USED TO PADDLING A SURFBOARD.

MY BEST WORD OF ADVICE TO THE NOVICE IS, *"**ENDURE.**"* THE MUSCLE ACHE AND BOARD RASH WILL FADE AND A STRONGER YOU WILL EMERGE **IF** YOU HAVE THE DETERMINATION TO ENDURE THE FIRST FEW SESSIONS.

YAH, I REMEMBA' WHEN I FIRST TRIED TO SURF...

PROPER PADDLING POSITION

HEAD UP — BEEG SMILE — ARCH BACK — FEET TOGETHER — SPACE — SMALL SPACE — CUPPED HANDS

WHEN PADDLING, REMEMBER TO ARCH YOUR BACK AND POSITION YOURSELF ON YOUR BOARD SO THAT THE NOSE IS BARELY OVER THE WATER. THE POSITION SHOWN ABOVE WILL GIVE YOU THE MOST SPEED WHILE USING THE LEAST AMOUNT OF ENERGY.

PRACTICE PADDLING OUT AND CATCHING WHITEWASH WAVES BACK TO SHORE ON YOUR BELLY. THIS WILL HELP YOU TO FIND YOUR SPOT ON THE BOARD. YOU WILL SEE THAT WHEN YOU ARE TOO FAR FORWARD YOU WILL NOSE DIVE OR *"PEARL"* IN FRONT OF THE WAVE. IF YOU ARE TOO FAR BACK YOU CANNOT GET INTO THE WAVE AND IT WILL PASS YOU BY.

CAUTION: AT THIS STAGE OF LEARNING YOU ARE AT YOUR MOST VULNERABLE AND MOST DANGEROUS STAGE OF THE GAME. BE EXTRA CAREFUL TO AVOID DANGEROUS SITUATIONS. LEARNING IS BEST DONE IN UNCROWDED SURF. USING A SOFT SURFBOARD WILL FURTHER LESSEN THE CHANCE OF INJURY TO YOURSELF AND OTHERS.

WHEN PADDLING BACK OUT

TRY AS MUCH AS POSSIBLE TO STAY CLEAR OF THE BREAKING WAVES. THIS IS TO AVOID INCOMING SURFERS AND ALSO TO KEEP FROM GETTING PUSHED BACK TO SHORE. OF COURSE, YOU CAN'T PADDLE AROUND EVERY WAVE.

SO WHAT HAPPENS WHEN A WAVE BREAKS IN FRONT OF YOU?

DO YOU THROW YOUR BOARD ON THE SIDE AND DIVE FOR DA REEF? YOU COULD, BUT THAT CAN BE DANGEROUS AS WELL AS FOOLISH. SOONER OR LATER YOU GOTTA LEARN TO **"DIP"** UNDER THE WAVES. HERE'S THREE EASY STEPS TO FOLLOW...

DA DIP

STEP 1) *AS THE BREAKING WAVE APPROACHES, PADDLE HARD STRAIGHT TOWARD IT. WHEN THE WAVE IS JUST A FEW FEET IN FRONT OF YOU, GRAB THE NOSE OF YOUR BOARD WITH BOTH HANDS AND PUSH IT UNDER THE WAVE AS HARD AS YOU CAN.*

STEP 2) *ONCE THE NOSE IS SUBMERGED, IMMEDIATELY PUSH THE TAIL OF THE BOARD DOWN WITH ONE OF YOUR FEET. NOW YOUR BOARD AND BODY ARE TOTALLY SUBMERGED.*

STEP 3) *WHEN THE WAVE PASSES OVER YOU, POINT THE NOSE UP TOWARD THE SKY, POP OUT THE BACK, AND CONTINUE PADDLING.*

GETTING UP

THE MOST IMPORTANT THING ABOUT CATCHING A WAVE IS BEING IN THE RIGHT POSITION. THE MORE EXPERIENCE YOU GET THE BETTER YOUR JUDGMENT WILL BECOME — **JUDGMENT** IS A **BIG** PART OF SURFING. IDEALLY, YOU WANT TO CATCH A WAVE JUST BEFORE IT BREAKS.

WHEN THE WAVE APPROACHES, PADDLE IN THE SAME DIRECTION WITH IT TO GAIN MOMENTUM. AS IT LIFTS YOU, TAKE A DEEP BREATH AND SHIFT YOUR WEIGHT FORWARD. SOMETIMES, A KICKING MOTION WILL HELP THRUST YOU INTO THE WAVE.

AT THIS POINT YOU ARE AT THE TOP OF THE WAVE AND IT'S PUSHING YOU FORWARD. IN ONE QUICK MOTION, PLACE YOUR HANDS ON YOUR BOARD JUST BELOW YOUR SHOULDERS AND PUSH YOURSELF UP INTO A STANDING POSITION.

ONLY EASY!

IT MAY TAKE MANY TRIES BEFORE YOU CAN STAND ON A SURFBOARD WITHOUT FALLING OFF. **KEEP TRYING.** "GETTING UP" ON A SURFBOARD WILL BE ONE OF THE GREATEST ACHIEVEMENTS IN YOUR LIFE!

CORRECT   **JUNK**

*BE SURE TO STAND WITH ONE FOOT FORWARD AND ONE BACK.
   HAVING BOTH FEET SIDE BY SIDE WILL GIVE YOU POOR BALANCE.

PLUS YOU GOIN' LOOK STUPID!

IF YOU PLACE YOUR LEFT
FOOT FORWARD YOU ARE A
REGULAR FOOT.

IF YOU PLACE YOUR RIGHT
FOOT FORWARD YOU ARE A
GOOFY FOOT.

THOUGH THE GOAL IN SURFING IS NOT TO **"WIPE OUT,"** IT IS OF COURSE, INEVITABLE. JUST CONSIDER IT PART OF PAYING YOUR DUES. WIPING OUT IS NOT NECESSARILY A BAD THING. IF YOU CAN LEARN TO ENJOY IT YOU WILL ACQUIRE A WEALTHY SOUL.

THE FORCE OF A WAVE CAN HOLD YOU UNDER WATER FOR WHAT SEEMS LIKE AN ETERNITY. YOU FEEL HELPLESS LIKE A SPECK OF SAND IN A WASHING MACHINE. BUT EH, **DON'T PANIC!**

WIPING OUT

IN REALITY YOU CAN HOLD YOUR BREATH LONGER THAN MOST ANY WAVE CAN HOLD YOU UNDER. JUST KEEP YOUR SENSES AND **GO WITH THE FLOW.** SCRAMBLING FOR THE SURFACE WHILE THE WAVE IS STILL CHURNING WILL ONLY WASTE YOUR VALUABLE OXYGEN.

REMEMBER, LET THE WAVE TAKE YOU AND KNOW THAT WHEN IT LETS GO YOU **WILL SURVIVE.**

DIS IS IT! *DA MOST CRITICAL PART OF A RIDE. THE OBJECT IS TO GET FROM THE TOP OF THE WAVE TO THE BOTTOM. IF YOU'RE STILL STANDIN'... YOU'VE MADE DA DROP. EVERY MOVE FROM HERE ON IS JUST A MATTER OF SHIFTING YOUR WEIGHT.*

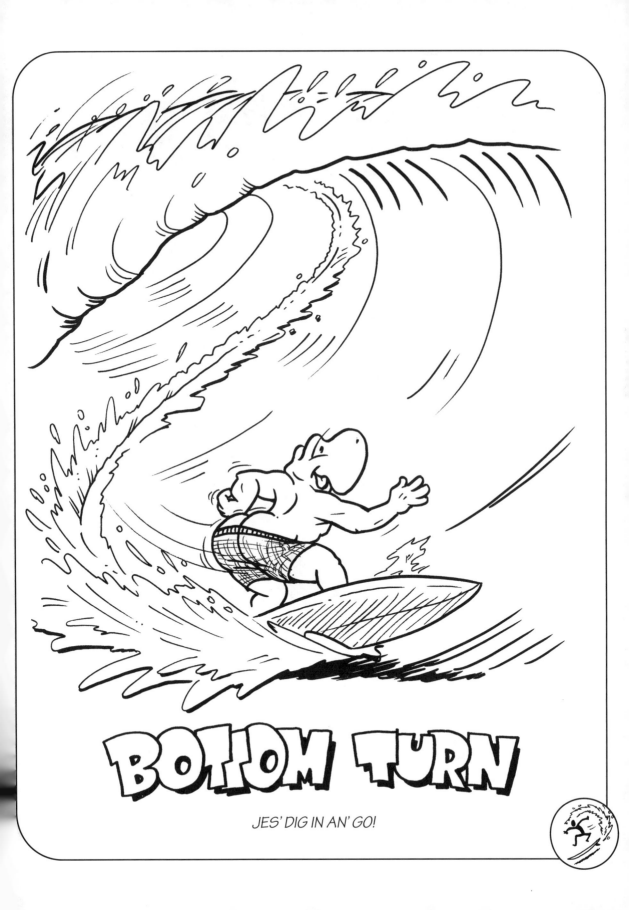

BOTTOM TURN

JES' DIG IN AN' GO!

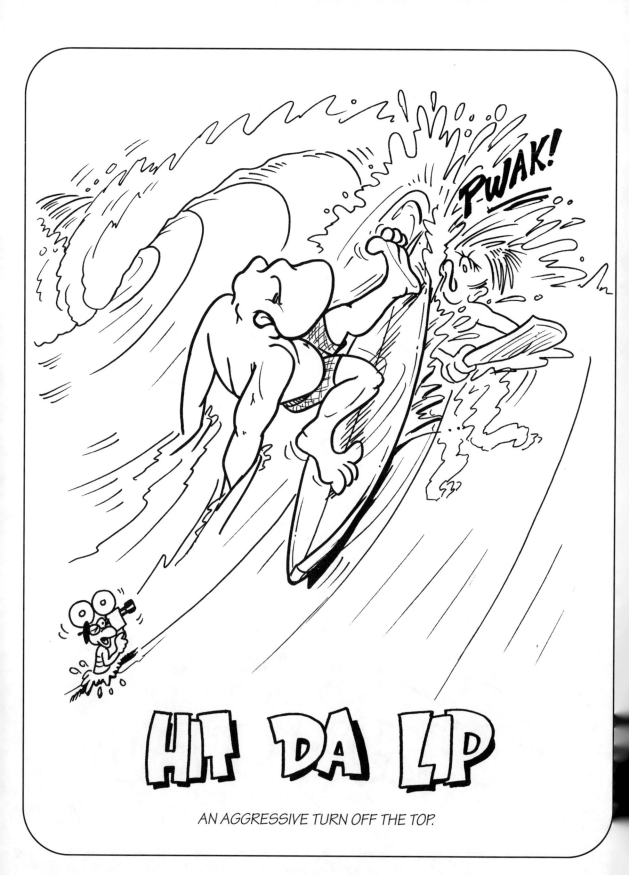

AN AGGRESSIVE TURN OFF THE TOP.

SWING IT AROUND AND GO BACK FOR MORE.

IN DA TUBE

SPEND AS MUCH TIME IN HERE AS YOU CAN. SCREAM A LOT — IT SOUNDS NEAT!

WHILE COASTING OVER A BROKEN SECTION OF WAVE ... THINK LIGHT.

THE ULTIMATE MOVE . . .

KA HULI NUI (THE BIG TURN OVER)

KICKING OUT

EXITING AT THE RIGHT TIME IS A LESSON
LEARNED FROM EXPERIENCE.

LONGBOARDING

THIS APPROACH TO SURFING ALLOWS FOR CREATIVE EXPRESSION THAT IS NOT AVAILABLE TO SHORTBOARDERS. LONGBOARDS ARE MORE BUOYANT AND STABLE, THEREBY ALLOWING SURFERS TO BE MORE CREATIVE IN THEIR MANEUVERS. "WALKING THE BOARD," "HANGING TEN" AND "TANDEM" SURFING ARE JUST A FEW MOVES POSSIBLE ON LONGER BOARDS.

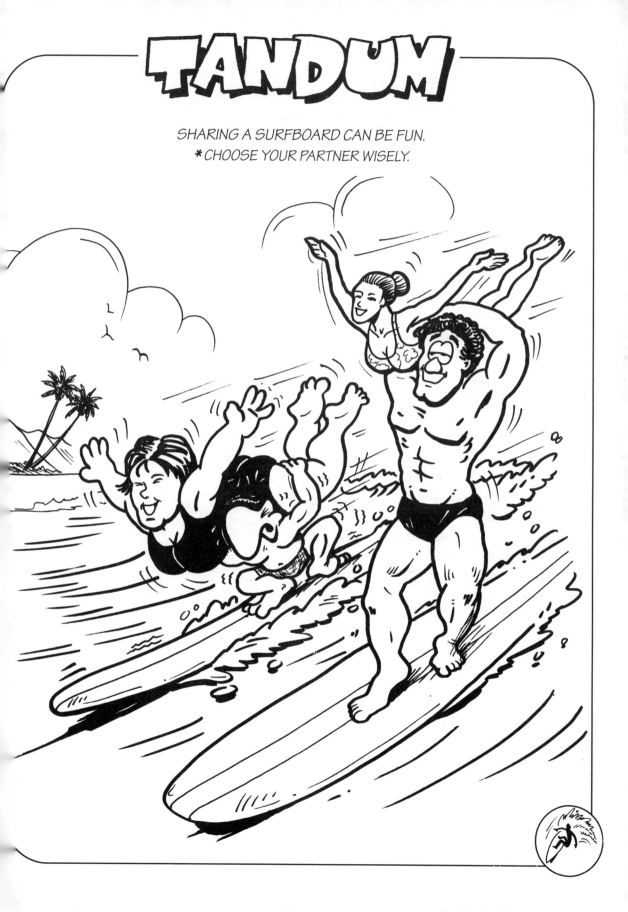

SURF EDAKET

SURFING HAS MANY UNWRITTEN LAWS. UNFORTUNATELY, EACH SURFER MUST DISCOVER THESE LAWS FOR HIMSELF. . . THEY ARE, AFTER ALL, UNWRITTEN.

UNWRITTEN LAWS OF SURFING

LAW #1)

LAW #2)

LAW #3)

LAW #4)

LAW # 5) * THIS ONE IS REALLY IMPORTANT

LAW

I *CAN* TELL YOU THAT IT'S NOT ENOUGH JUST TO KNOW HOW TO SURF. SURVIVING IN THE CROWDED, AND OFTEN COMPETITIVE, SURF REQUIRES AN UNDERSTANDING OF SURFING EDAKET.

BE RESPECTFUL OF YOUR FELLOW SURFERS. WE'RE ALL OUT THERE TO ENJOY DA OCEAN.

IN UDDUH WERDS, YOU GOTTA KNOW HOW FO' ACT! -

THERE'S AN OBVIOUS ORDER IN WHICH SURFERS AT A GIVEN SPOT LINE UP TO AWAIT INCOMING WAVES. USUALLY THE BEST, MOST RESPECTED, OR JUST PLAIN **BIGGEST** SURFERS ARE IN THE BEST POSITION AND THEREFORE GET MOST OF THE WAVES.

— BUT RIPPA'S, LET DA GREMMIES CATCH WAVES TOO AH!

ONE IMPORTANT THING TO REMEMBER IS . . . WHOEVER STANDS UP FIRST, IN THE MOST CRITICAL PART OF THE WAVE, HAS THE RIGHT OF WAY. IT'S NOT NICE TO TAKE OFF IN FRONT OF (OR "DROP IN" ON) THAT PERSON.

SURF HAZARDS

SUNBURN: *SKIN TURNS RED, HOT, SORE; MAY BLISTER. LIPS MAY CRACK AND EVENTUALLY PEEL OFF.*

TREATMENT: *PREVENTION — USE WATERPROOF SUNSCREEN AND LIP BALM. THE JUICE FROM THE ALOE PLANT IS GREAT FOR SOOTHING BURNS. JES' RUB IT ON.*

BOARD RASH: *IF YOUR SKIN IS NOT USED TO THE FRICTION CAUSED BY SURF WAX, IT WILL TURN RED. YOUR RIBS MAY FEEL BRUISED AS WELL.*

SHORTS RASH: *THE GIRLS DON'T KNOW, BUT THE LITTLE BOYS UNDERSTAND.*

TREATMENT: *THIS WILL FADE AS YOU GET USED TO THE FRICTION. SOAP & WATER OR ALOE MAY HELP.*

WANA: (VAH-NAH) *SEA URCHIN. THE SPINES WILL BREAK OFF IN YOUR FEET IF YOU STEP ON THESE.*

TREATMENT: *IT MAY SEEM REPULSIVE, BUT SOAKING THE AFFECTED AREA IN SHI-SHI WILL DISSOLVE THE EMBEDDED SPINES.*

PO'DAGEE MAN O WAR: *A TYPE OF FLOATING JELLYFISH THAT STINGS REAL BAD.*

TREATMENT: *COVER AFFECTED AREA WITH A PASTE OF MEAT TENDERIZER AND WATER, OR THE WHITE SAP FROM A GREEN PAPAYA. CALL A DOCTOR AND WATCH FOR ALLERGIC REACTION.*

BLACK EYE: *MAY BE CAUSED BY CRASHING INTO SOMEONE BIGGER THAN YOU.*

TREATMENT: *THESE USUALLY FADE IN A WEEK OR SO. ICE AND SUNGLASSES MAY HELP.*

SORE MUSCLES: *ESPECIALLY NECK, SHOULDER AND BACK. MORE COMMON WITH BEGINNERS.*

TREATMENT: *TOUGH IT OUT! THE PAIN WILL EASE AS YOUR BODY GETS USED TO TWISTING AND PADDLING.*

KAKIOS: (KAH-KEE-OHS)
VARIOUS SCRAPES, CUTS AND GASHES ACQUIRED BY BOUNCING OFF DA REEF. A.K.A. REEF RASH.

TREATMENT: *CLEAN REEF CUTS WELL, THEY ARE EASILY INFECTED. SEE A DOCTOR.*

DINGS:
PUKAS OR DENTS IN SURF-BOARD FROM CONTACT WITH REEF, BODY PARTS, OTHER BOARDS, OR FORGETTING TO STRAP YOUR BOARD TO THE SURF RACKS.

TREATMENT: *CAN BE FIXED WIT FOAM, FIBERGLASS AND RESIN. DO **NOT** CALL A DOCTOR.*

WHAT ABOUT

SHARKS LIVE IN THE OCEAN. THEY HAVE FOR MILLIONS OF YEARS. THE ONLY GUARANTEE' WAY TO AVOID SHARKS IS TO STAY OUT OF THE OCEAN.

MOST SHARKS WILL NOT BOTHER HUMANS; HOWEVER, THEY ARE NOTORIOUSLY UNPREDICTABLE. DON'T BELIEVE ANYONE WHO CLAIMS TO KNOW EVERYTHING ABOUT SHARKS.

GUIDELINES TO LOWER THE RISK OF SHARK ATTACK:

1) DON'T SURF BEFORE SUNRISE OR AFTER SUNSET.

2) DON'T SURF NEAR RIVER MOUTHS OR HARBOR ENTRANCES.

3) DON'T SURF IN MURKY WATER.

4) DON'T SURF ALONE OR IN SMALL GROUPS.

IN UDDUH WORDS: AVOID ALL THE BEST SPOTS AND CONDITIONS IF YOU' WORRIED ABOUT SHARKS!

AN' DON'T BELIEVE THAT STUFF ABOUT SHARKS ATTACKING SURFA'S 'CAUSE THEY LOOK LIKE TURTLES OR SEALS. I THINK THEY ATTACK TURTLES AND SEALS 'CAUSE THEY LOOK LIKE SURFA'S!

SEAL

TURTLE

SURFA'

SHARK'S EYE VIEW

HOW FO' TALK
(SURF SLANG GLOSSARY)

BAD: GOOD.

BARREL: TUBE, PIPE, THE HOLLOW PART OF A WAVE.

BRAH: SHORT FOR BRUDDUH OR BROTHER. NOT WOMEN'S UNDERWEAR.

DING: PUKA OR DENT IN YOUR BOARD; ALSO, SOUND YOU HEAR BEFORE "DONG."

FRONTSIDE: SURFING WITH THE FRONT OF YOUR BODY TOWARD THE WAVE.
OPPOSITE OF **BACKSIDE:** SURFING WITH YOUR BACK TOWARD THE WAVE.

GONZO: ENTHUSIASTIC, READY FOR ACTION.

GRIND: 1. TO EAT VORACIOUSLY. 2. TO "EAT IT" OR WIPE OUT.

GARENS ALSO **GARENS BALLBARENS:** GUARANTEE(D), A SURE THING.

GREMMIE: GEEK, NURD, IDIOT, OR BEGINNER.

HOO-TA! ALSO **BANZAI!** OR **AHHHH!:** EXCLAMATIONS OF ELATION UTTERED JUST BEFORE TAKE OFF, IMPACT AND/OR POSSIBLE DEATH.

LINE UP: THE TAKE-OFF AREA WHERE SURFERS GATHER TO CATCH WAVES.

LOKOS: REGULARS OR RESIDENTS OF A GIVEN LOCATION OR SURF SPOT.

LŌLŌ: (LOW-LOW) REFERS TO ONE WHO IS NOT ALL THERE. YOU KNOW, LIGHTS ON BUT NOBODY HOME?

MENTO: MENTALLY LACKING, LŌLŌ.

ONREAL: NOT REAL OR SEEMINGLY IMPOSSIBLE.

OVER THE FALLS: TO BE SUCKED UP AND OVER A WAVE THEN DRIVEN UNDER AND SWIRLED AROUND. THIS MAY BE REPEATED SEVERAL TIMES.

PEARL: SHORT FOR "PEARL DIVE;" TO NOSE UNDER AND GRIND ESPECIALLY WHILE TAKING THE DROP.

PO'DAGEE ALSO **POCHO:** PORTUGUESE MAN-O-WAR OR JUST PORTUGUESE IN GENERAL.

PUKA: HOLE, PUNCTURE.

PUMPEN': PUMPING. AS IN "DA WAVES IS PUMPEN'!"

RAD: SHORT FOR RADICAL. SAME AS BAD (MEANING GOOD).

SETS: (NOT SEX!) OFTEN SCREAMED BY SURFERS AS SETS OF WAVES APPROACH.

SHAKA: AWESOME, RIGHT ON, RIGHTEOUS, FAR OUT AND SOLID.

SHI-SHI: URINE, NUMBER 1.

'KAY-DEN: WELL OKAY THEN, SEE YOU LATER, FAREWELL, THAT'S A WRAP, ALOHA, SAYONADA, DA RIVA DIRTY, I'LL BE DA SAME!

PALAKA JOE'S WISE WORDS

— *WHERE EVA' YOU STAY . . . DAS' WHERE YOU ARE . . .*
  (MAKE THE BEST OF YOUR SITUATION)

— *WHAT EVA' HAPPENS IN DA SURF, YOU WILL*$_\wedge$*SURVIVE*
                                                    PROBABLY
  (EVERYTHING WILL$_\wedge$BE ALL RIGHT)
              PROBABLY

— *NO PANIC IN DA OCEAN.*
  (KEEP YOUR HEAD — USE IT TO THINK WITH)

— *DA OCEAN IS AN EMPTY CANVASS . . . NO MO' RULES!*
  (BE CREATIVE . . . ANYTHING'S POSSIBLE)

— *CLOSE YO' EYE, NO SCA'DE DIE, GOTTA TRY,
  NOT BUMBUY!*
        (NOTHING VENTURED NOTHING GAINED —
              GO FOR IT NOW!)

  AN' LASS BUT NOT LEAST . . .

  TODAY . . . IS TOMORROW'S . . . YESTA'DAY
  (SEIZE THE MOMENT)

DASS DEEP!

AND NOW WATERBUG...

*YOU HAVE EVOLVED INTO A BEAUTIFUL WAVE RIDER.
I HAVE GIVEN YOU THE KNOWLEDGE YOU NEED TO
NAVIGATE YOUR WAY THROUGH THE SETS OF LIFE.
IT'S UP TO YOU NOW, WATERBUG. GO. GO AND SEEK
OUT THE WAVE OF LIFE. RIDE IT. BECOME ONE WITH IT.
NEVER LOOK BACK. THE FUTURE IS IN YOUR HANDS...*

START PADDLING!

PATRICK CHING AND JEFF PAGAY

WERE BORN AND RAISED IN HAWAI'I. THEY BEEN BUDDIES SINCE THE SEVENTH GRADE. BOTH GRADUATED FROM MOANALUA HIGH SCHOOL, PATRICK IN 1980, AND JEFF IN 1981. THROUGH THE YEARS THEY BEEN THROUGH COUNTLESS LŌLŌ ADVENTURES, MANY OF WHICH THEY RECORDED AS CARTOONS. THEIR LOVE OF ART, HUMOR, AND OF COURSE SURFING HAS BEEN A COMMON BOND IN THEIR LIVES.

TODAY **PATRICK** IS A NOTED WILDLIFE ARTIST AND AUTHOR OF SEVERAL BOOKS ON HAWAIIAN ANIMALS. HE HAS BEEN DRAWING PALAKA JOE SINCE THE SECOND GRADE.

JEFF SPECIALIZES IN AIRBRUSH ART AND HAS PRODUCED ALBUM COVERS, MURALS, LOGOS AND COUNTLESS CUSTOM T-SHIRTS. HE ALSO TEACHES SUNDAY SCHOOL AND PLAYS IN A CHRISTIAN ROCK BAND.

SUPA' GONZO MAHALO

TO ALL WHO HELPED MAKE DIS BOOK HAPPEN. SPECIAL THANKS TO RELL SUNN AND DAVE PARMENTER FOR THEIR CONTRIBUTION TO THE BOOK AND TO THE SPORT OF SURFING, PHYLLIS SEGAWA FOR HER HELP, ENCOURAGEMENT AND ALL HER SCOLDINGS, BARBARA POPE AND HER BOOK DESIGN STAFF, AND MAILE MEYER FOR MARKETING ADVICE.

THANKS ALSO TO KRISTEN HEISE (HI-Z) FOR HER CARICATURES OF PATRICK, JEFF AND RELL, AND ALL YOU CHARACTERS IN THE SURF WHO INSPIRED THE CHARACTERS IN THIS BOOK.

IF DIS BOOK OFFENDS YOU...

RELAX!
IT'S JES' ONE
KA'TOON!

IN MEMORY *OF THE LATE JUDGE BARRY J. RUBIN WHO HELPED ME IN MANY WAYS AND GAVE ME THE IDEA TO DO THIS BOOK SO MANY YEARS AGO.*

ALOHA BARRY, Patrick

ALSO DEDICATED *TO MY DAD, LARRY PAGAY, WHO IS HOME WITH THE LORD. HE ENCOURAGED MY ART, LOVED SURFING IN EARLIER YEARS, AND STRENGTHENED MY FAITH IN GOD.*

YOUR SON, Jeff

Published by NATURALLY HAWAIIAN
1476 Ala Hekili Place, Honolulu, HI 96819
ISBN 0-89610-306-4
PRINTED IN THE U.S.A.